Weather

by Nan Walker

Scholastic Inc.
New York Toronto London Auckland
Sydney Mexico City New Delhi Hong Kong

Created by Q2AMedia
Designers Neha Kaul, Ritu Chopra and Joita Das
Art Director Sumit Charles

Picture Credits:
t=top, b=bottom, r= right, l= left

Cover Page: Peter Gudella: Shutterstock, Holly Sisson: Istockphoto, Brykaylo Yuriy: Shutterstock, David Franklin: Istockphoto.

Back Cover: Marilyn Nieves: Istockphoto.

Title Page: Gorilla: Shutterstock.

Imprint Page: Michael William: Shutterstock.

Interior: 4 Grafica: Shutterstock. 5t Dmitriy Eremenkov: Shutterstock. 5b Maszas: Shutterstock. 5, 9, 15, 17, 19, 23: Shutterstock. 6 Photobank.Kiev.Ua: Shutterstock. 9l, 23t Christophe Testi: Shutterstock. 9r Lofoto: Shutterstock. 10 Rudy Umans: Shutterstock. 11t JenniferPhotographyImaging: Istockphoto. 11b James Steidl: Dreamstime. 12 Jeremy Mayes: Istockphoto. 14 Zurijeta: Shutterstock. 15 Leslie Miller: Photolibrary. 16 Dmitry Naumov: Shutterstock. 17t Ernest Washington: Photolibrary. 17b Richard Goldberg: Shutterstock. 18 Danijel Micka: Dreamstime. 19 Trudy Wilkerson: Shutterstock. 20 Linda Kloosterhof: Istockphoto. 20-21 German: Istockphoto, Toponium: Shutterstock . 22 Javier Larrea: Photolibrary. 23 Shane White: Shutterstock, Design: Shutterstock, Parfta: Shutterstock.

Q2AMedia Art Bank : 7, 8.

No part of this publication may be reproduced, stored in a retrieval system, or transmitted in any form or by any means, electronic, mechanical, photocopying, recording, or otherwise, without written permission of the publisher. For information regarding permission, write to Scholastic Inc., Attention: Permissions Department, 557 Broadway, New York, NY 10012.

ISBN 978-0-545-27360-2

Copyright © 2010 by Scholastic Inc.
All rights reserved. Published by Scholastic Inc.

SCHOLASTIC and associated logos are trademarks and/or registered trademarks of Scholastic Inc.

12 11 10 9 8 7 6 5 4 3 2 1   10 11 12 13 14 15/0

Printed and assembled in China

Contents

Introduction	4
The Four Seasons	6
Day and Night	8
Sky Full of Clouds	10
The Water Cycle	12
What's the Temperature?	14
Rain or Snow	16
Windy Days	18
How's the Weather?	20
Weather Watchers	22
Glossary	24

What is the weather like today?

Take a look outside. Is it wet and wild, or easy breezy? Is it cold as an icicle or hot enough to fry an egg on the sidewalk?

Some days, the weather seems like a sunny friend. Other times, it is like an angry enemy.

What makes the weather change from day to day? Where does weather come from, anyway?

Believe it or not, weather starts very, very far away. It starts with the sun!

FAST FACT

How far is the sun from Earth? It is about 93 million miles (150 million kilometers) away. If you could drive a car in space, a trip to the sun would take more than 160 years!

Thermometer Activity

This book includes a model thermometer. Slide the arrow up and down. Do you see changes in the thermometer? The higher you move the arrow, the higher the temperature it shows. As you read the book, look for this thermometer symbol. That means you'll need to use the model thermometer for an activity.

The Four Seasons

In many parts of the world, every year brings a chilly winter, hot summer, and warm spring and fall. Have you ever wondered why there are four seasons?

It is all because of Earth's relationship with the sun.

The sun is very, very hot, and it provides Earth with heat and light.

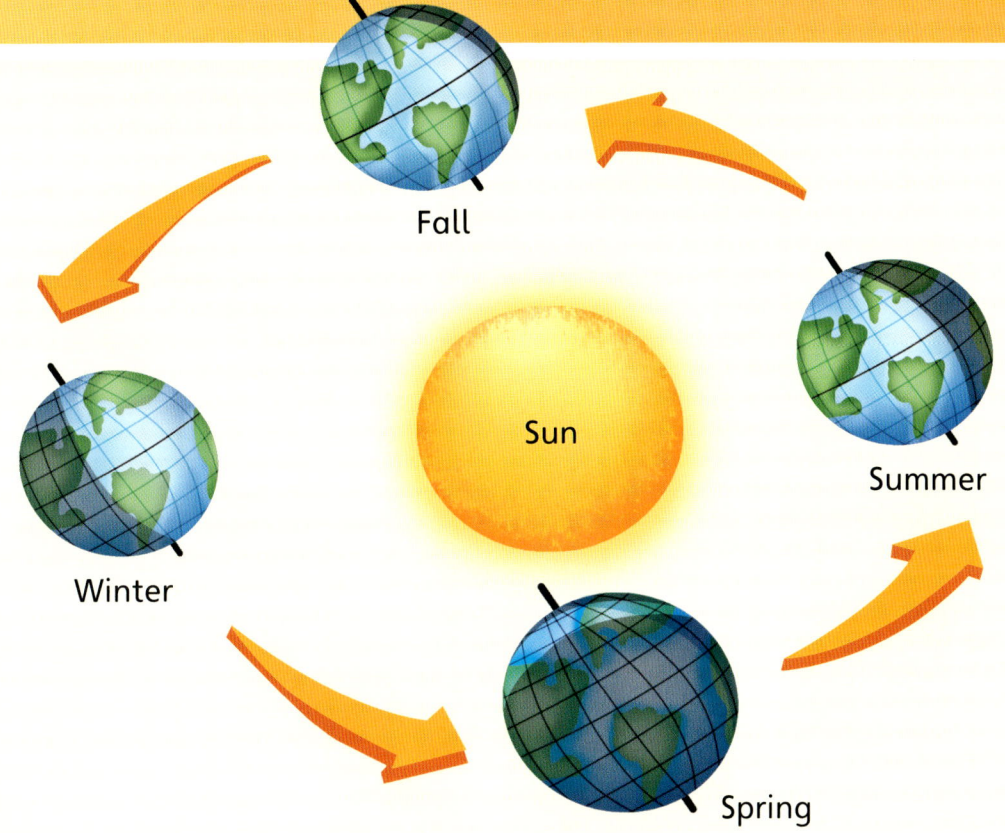

Earth **revolves** around the sun. Every year, or 365 days, the planet completes one trip around the sun.

As Earth travels, it tilts. That causes different parts of Earth to receive more sunlight at different times of a year.

When the part of Earth where you live is tilted toward the sun, you get more heat and light. You experience summer. When your part of Earth tilts away from the sun, winter occurs. In between come spring and fall.

Day and Night

A sunny day turns into a chilly night. Where did the sun go?

While Earth loops around the sun, it also **rotates**. Earth makes one complete spin in a day, or 24 hours.

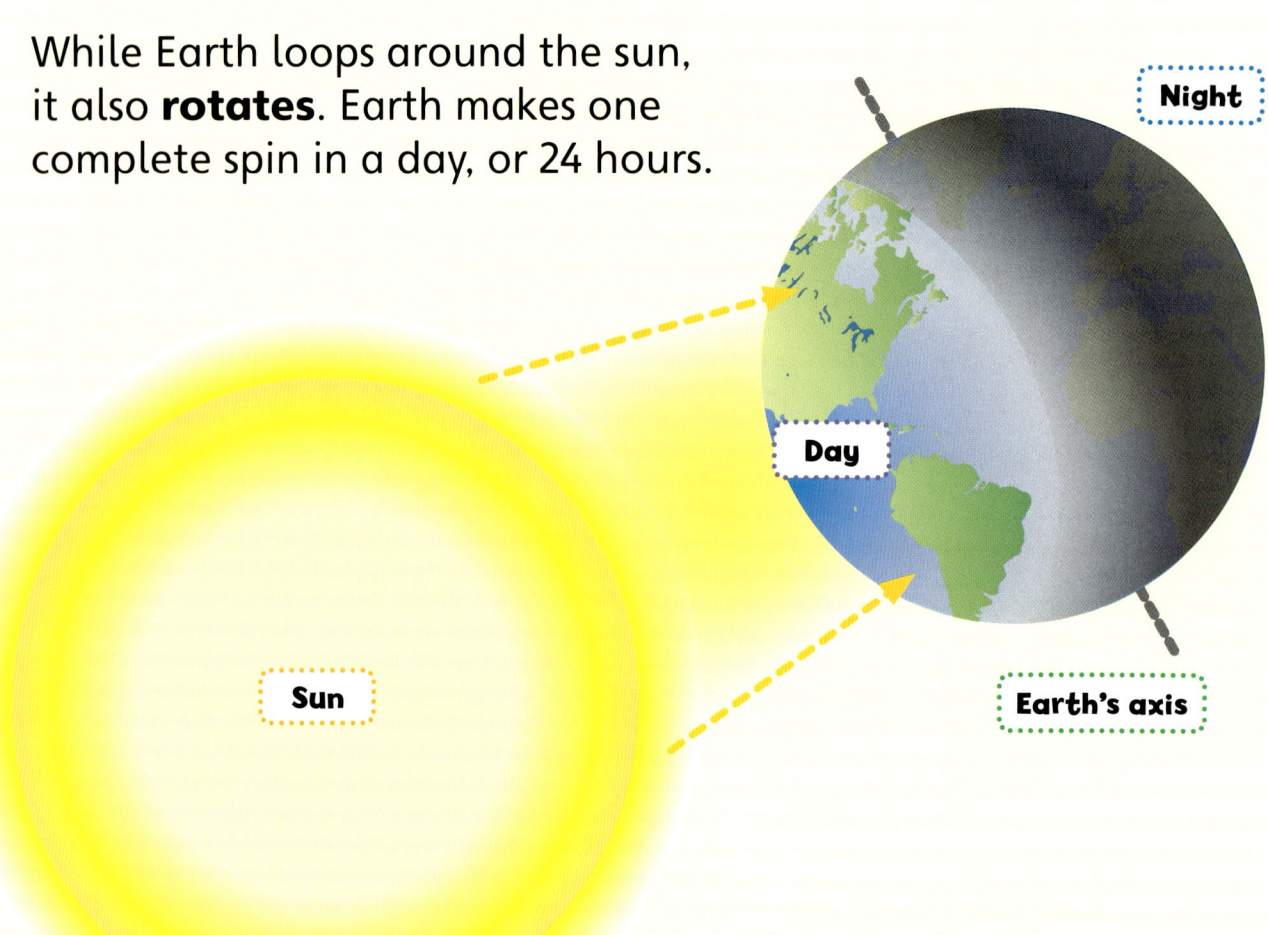

When your side of Earth turns toward the sun, it is daytime. When your side turns away from the sun, it is night.

But even in the daytime, you can't always see the sun. Sometimes clouds get in the way.

Hands-on Activity

If you have a globe, try this! Put your finger on the location where you live. Now put your finger on the opposite side of the globe. When it is day for you, it is night for the people on the other side of Earth!

Thermometer Activity

In the Sahara Desert, temperatures can reach a scorching 113°F (45°C) during the day and drop to 23°F (-5°C) at night. Find the day temperature on your thermometer. Now move the marker down to the night temperature. That's a big difference!

Sky Full of Clouds

Clouds may look as soft and fluffy as a pillow. But if you tried to rest on one, you would fall right through!

Clouds are not **solid**. They are made of very tiny drops of water or ice **crystals**. There are many different types of clouds. Let's learn about the main types!

Cirrus clouds

Cirrus clouds are thin and wispy. They look like curls of hair! These clouds appear high in the sky. You can usually see them on a clear day.

Stratus clouds

Stratus clouds spread out in a thin layer. They hang low in the sky. Sometimes these clouds bring drizzle.

Cumulus clouds

Cumulus clouds are puffy, like a head of cauliflower. When they grow big and dark, a storm is on the way!

The Water Cycle

Why are there clouds in the sky? Clouds are part of the **water cycle**.

Water travels from land to sky, and back again. Earth uses the same water again and again! Let's learn how the water cycle works.

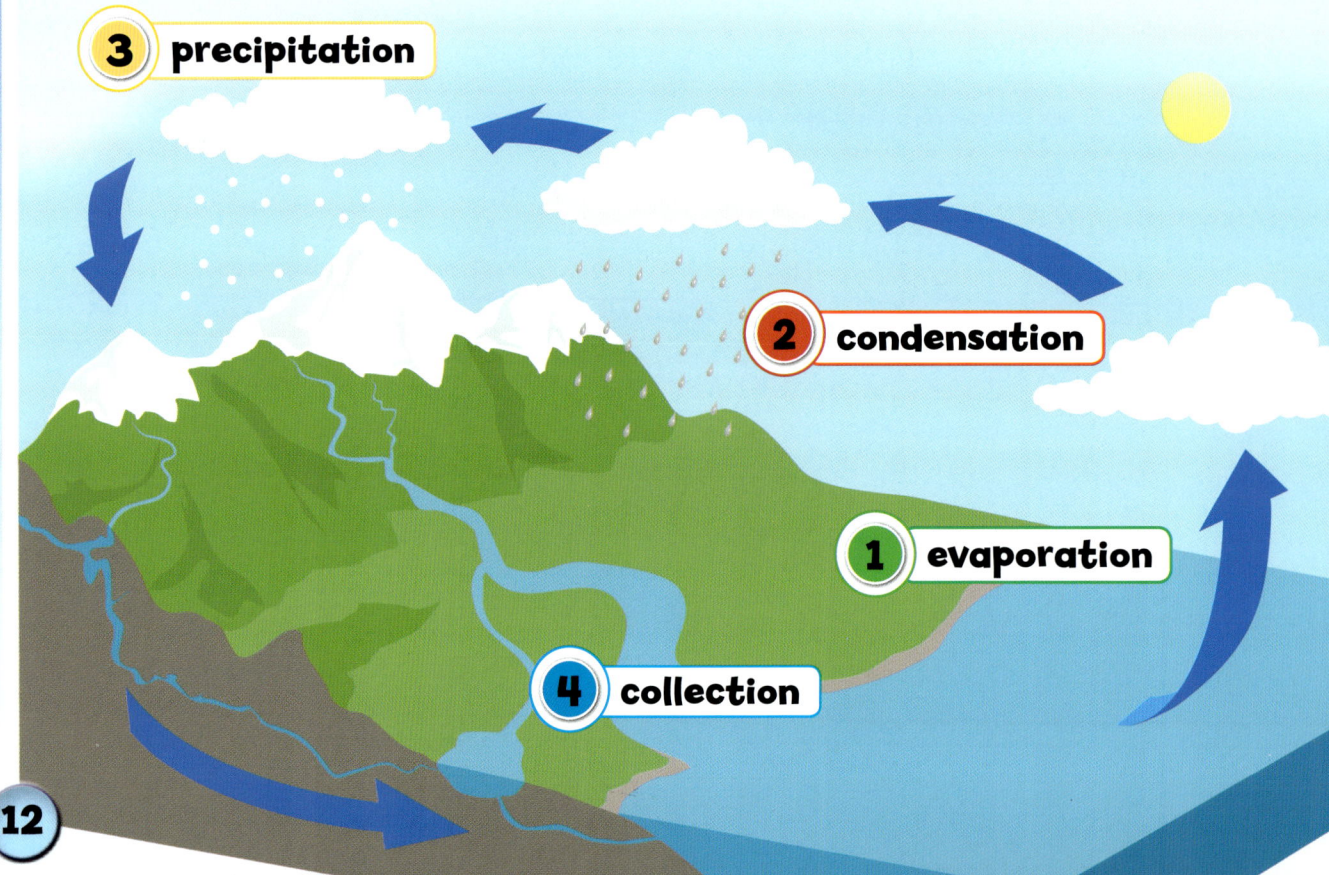

1

The sun heats water on Earth's surface. That includes oceans, lakes, or even a puddle. Water **evaporates**, turning into **vapor** that rises into the air.

2

High up in the sky, the air is cooler than on the ground. As the vapor cools, it **condenses** and forms clouds.

3

More water joins the cloud. The cloud becomes too heavy with water. What happens next? Grab your umbrella! The water comes down as **precipitation**.

4

Water flows into oceans, ponds, and lakes. The water cycle begins again!

What's the Temperature?

Will rain or snow fall from the sky? That depends on the temperature. You use a thermometer to tell how hot or cold it is.

The symbol ° means "degree."

Temperature is measured in degrees. It can be measured in degrees Fahrenheit (°F) or degrees Celsius (°C).

FAST FACT

Most countries in the world, including Canada, measure temperature in Celsius. The United States measures temperature in Fahrenheit.

Thermometer Activity

Move the marker on your thermometer to 72°F (22°C). This is the average **room temperature**. At around this temperature, you feel comfortable indoors. Move the marker to 32°F (0°C). This is the **freezing point**. At this temperature or cooler, water freezes into a solid like ice or snow.

Rain or Snow

High up in the clouds, the air is usually below freezing. Guess what happens to the water droplets in these types of clouds? They freeze into ice crystals. Snowflakes are made of clusters of ice crystals.

When this frozen precipitation falls toward the ground, it could stay as snow, or turn into rain or sleet. How? Let's find out!

Snow

On the trip down from clouds to the ground, the ice crystals travel through air temperatures that are at or below freezing point. The crystals stay frozen as snow.

Rain

The ice crystals travel through air that is above the freezing point. They melt into rain.

Sleet

The snow first falls through a layer of warm air. The ice crystals melt into rain. Then, the rain meets freezing temperatures near the ground. The rain freezes into small chunks of ice.

Thermometer Activity

Move the marker on your thermometer to 60°F (15°C). At that temperature, will it rain or snow?

Now move the marker to 20°F (-7°C). Will it rain or snow?

Windy Days

As you learned, warm air mixed with cold air can bring wild weather. Sometimes, it even causes wind!

Wind occurs when the sun's heat warms Earth's surface. Hot air is lighter than cold air, so it rises. Heavier cool air rushes to fill the empty space left behind by the rising hot air. This moving air is wind.

Ahhh! On a hot day, the wind can cool you off.

Brrrr! On a cold day, the wind can make you even colder. The harder it blows, the colder you feel.

Sometimes, a heavy snowstorm comes with very strong winds. This is called a **blizzard**. The blowing snow can be so strong that you can hardly see what's around you.

The winds blow the snow into **drifts**. These snow piles can reach several feet high. Sometimes, they can be even taller than you!

Thermometer Activity

Move your thermometer marker to 40°F (-4°C). A breeze can make it feel as if it is 35°F (2°C). A strong wind can make it feel like only 25°F (-4°C)!

How's the Weather?

It may be snowing where you live, but it could be sunny across the country.

Different places experience different kinds of weather. In North America, it is usually colder in the North and hotter in the South.

Look at this winter weather map. Use the key to answer the questions on the next page.

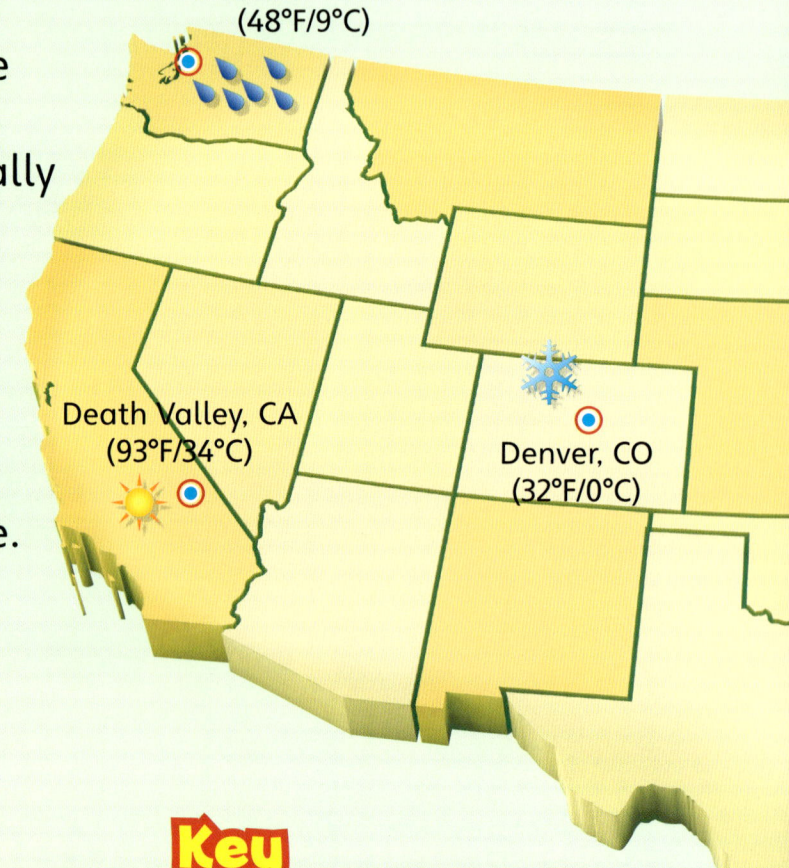

Seattle, WA (48°F/9°C)

Death Valley, CA (93°F/34°C)

Denver, CO (32°F/0°C)

Death Valley
Death Valley is a desert. It is hot and dry. In summer, it can get hotter than 120°F (49°C).

Key
Wind Snow Rain Sunshine

Chicago
Chicago is nicknamed the Windy City. In fact, it isn't any windier than many other American cities. But in winter, the wind can be bitterly cold.

Miami
In the winter of 2010, Florida had a big surprise—snow! The last time it snowed in Miami was in 1977.

Portland, ME (19°F/-7°C)
Boston, MA (23°F/-5°C)
Chicago, IL (23°F/-5°C)
Cleveland OH (30°F/-1°C)
New Orleans, LA (63°F/17°C)
Miami, FL (75°F/24°C)

Questions:

1. Where is it snowing?
2. Where is it raining?
3. What is the temperature in Miami, Florida?
4. What is the temperature in Portland, Maine?

Weather Watchers

Scientists who study the weather are called **meteorologists**. They use computers and scientific instruments to track the changes in the weather.

You can be a weather watcher, too! Make a chart like the one below.

My Weather Chart

	Temperature	The weather today is
Sunday		
Monday		
Tuesday		
Wednesday		
Thursday		
Friday		
Saturday		

Every day, have an adult help you study a real thermometer. Record the day's temperature in your chart. Write down what the weather is like each day, too.

Hands-on Activity

A **rain gauge** is an instrument that measures how much rain has fallen. Make your own rain gauge!

You Need: plastic ruler, glass jar, clear tape

To Do: Stand the ruler in the jar. Use tape to attach it to the jar.

Put the jar out in the open, away from trees or roofs.

After it rains, study the ruler to see how many inches (or centimeters) of rain fell.

Words to Use

Cloudy	Snowy
Cold	Sunny
Hot	Warm
Rainy	Windy

Thermometer Activity

After you record the real temperature each day, see if you can find the same temperature on your model thermometer.

Glossary

Blizzard Heavy snowstorm with high winds

Crystal Solid formed by an organized pattern of tiny particles called atoms

Condense To turn vapor or gas into liquid

Drift Bank or pile of drifted snow

Evaporate To turn liquid into vapor or gas

Freezing point Temperature at which water freezes, 32°F or 0°C

Meteorologist Scientist who studies the weather

Revolve To move around a central object

Room temperature Temperature at which humans feel comfortable indoors

Rotate To turn around on an axis or center

Solid Substance with weight and volume

Precipitation Water that falls as rain or snow to Earth's surface

Rain gauge Instrument that measures how much rain has fallen

Vapor Water that has turned into steam

Water cycle Earth's continuous recycling of its water supply